THE STORY OF THE WHEEL

FORDS PRAIRIE SCHOOL

The Story of the Wheel

by Walter Buehr

26720

G. P. PUTNAM'S SONS   NEW YORK

Text and illustrations © 1960 by Walter Buehr   All rights reserved
Library of Congress Catalogue Card Number: 60-12520
Manufactured in the United States of America
Published simultaneously in the Dominion of Canada by Longmans, Green and Company

BEFORE THE WHEEL

This is the story of the wheel and how it has changed all our lives. Try to imagine what it would be like today if the wheel had not been invented. If you live in a city there would be no streets, only narrow paths, because there would be no cars, trucks or even wagons. At night it would be pitch-dark, without electric lights. People would have to hold up burning torches to light their way. There would be no big stores, movie theaters, restaurants or banks. There would be no gas or electric stoves; all cooking would be done over a wood-burning fireplace which also heated the hut.

If you wanted to take a trip you would walk, or ride a horse or donkey, or maybe a camel. There would be no cars, trains, buses, planes, or steamships. You couldn't telegraph or phone, and of course there would be no radio or TV. Food would be a big problem. Grocers would have no frozen or canned foods on their shelves. They could only carry foods raised on farms close by. Cities in the North would never see an orange or a pineapple. In the South nobody would know what iced drinks or ice cream tasted like.

All food would have to be carried from farm to town on the farmer's back or on a pack horse or donkey, so the farms would have to be very near the city. In winter there would be no fresh fruits or vegetables at all.

If bad weather or insects ruined the crops near your city it would probably mean famine next winter. Even if there was plenty of food in another state only five hundred miles away, there would be no way to bring it before it rotted.

If you needed clothing you would have to trade for skins brought in by hunters or wear homespun woven from thread twisted by hand. It would take many days to make enough cloth on the crude hand loom for a coat.

In the country only rough paths would connect the little farms. Farmers could raise only small crops because their plowing, harrowing, cultivating and harvesting would all have to be done by hand, with spades, hoes, rakes and sickles.

You and your friends would probably live your whole lives without ever traveling more than a few short miles from your birthplace.

3

AMERICA WOULD LOOK LIKE THIS TODAY WITHOUT THE WHEEL

The best way to find out what your life would be like without the wheel is to see how the North American Indian lived before the white men arrived. There was not a single foot of road in all the trackless forests of America, only narrow paths and game trails. When the Indian moved he had to walk, carrying all his possessions·on his back. Only over the water could he ride, in a canoe made by hollowing out a log with fire and sharp shells, or by covering a

wooden frame with birch bark, made watertight by daubing the seams with pitch.

He had few tools, and these were made of stone, wood, or shell. His hut was built by sticking branches into the ground, bending them into a frame and covering it with bark or grasses. The Indian lived mostly on game and fish and had a few vegetables like corn and beans he raised on small cleared patches in the forest. Whatever he couldn't eat at once, he dried in the sun or smoked over a fire so it could be stored without spoiling. Often, in winter, all the dried food was eaten up. Then, unless the hunters found game, the tribe might starve before spring.

For clothes the red man wore the skins of animals he had killed. They were cured and sewn together by the squaws with thread made from the sinews of the animals. The women also wove crude blankets of shredded bark or grasses on primitive looms. This was life without the wheel.

TRAVEL BEFORE THE WHEEL

Here are some of the ways men traveled before the wheel. In India elephants were trained to carry people and freight on their backs. In places like India and Burma, elephants are still used to bring big logs out of the jungle.

The Arabs have used camel caravans to transport their goods across the desert for centuries; they still do. In the far north of Sweden the Lapps hitch reindeer to their sledges in the winter. During the Dark Ages in Europe roads were so poor that travelers all rode horseback and carried their baggage on pack horses or donkeys. In the big cities, nobles were carried about the town in sedan chairs.

6

EARLY USE OF THE WHEEL

The very first wheels were probably slabs of tree trunk, with holes bored through the center. Later they were made of planks nailed together with wooden pins and rounded by chopping or sawing. A wooden pin driven through a hole in the end of the axle kept the wheel from slipping off. The oxcart at lower right has such wheels.

The Greeks used chariots in battle. Sometimes their wheels were fitted with sharp blades that whirled around as the wheels turned, and cut down the enemy. At upper right are two eighteenth-century carriages. One is a two-wheeler and the other a high-wheel C-spring barouche. The craft with a sail is a Chinese wheelbarrow.

THE WHEEL IN TRANSPORTATION

Nobody knew who built the first wheel, or when. Probably some skin-clad, bearded cave men were dragging home the body of a huge cave bear they had killed with clubs and spears. Along the way they pulled it across a fallen log. The log began to roll and suddenly the load was easier to pull. They had discovered the roller!

The roller was used in many places. Egyptian picture writing shows great blocks of stone to be used in building the pyramids being dragged along over rollers. Until lately houses were moved to new sites by putting heavy beams under them and pulling them along the street over wooden rollers.

The trouble with rollers was that you had to keep picking them up from behind the skid and carrying them ahead and laying them down again. Finally some bright workman thought of putting an axle through the center of a large roller and fastening the ends of the axle to the skid. Thus the roller would always stay under the skid. He soon saw that he didn't need a solid wide roller. Two narrow ones connected by an axle did the job — and there were wheels!

But there were no roads, only paths for horsemen. No bridges spanned the rivers, only fords where horses could splash across.

So began the road-building age. It is still

going on today in the form of superhighways and throughways. At first roads were simply made by filling in holes and digging out boulders. In the spring when the ground was thawing or during heavy rains the mud kept the roads closed for months.

Little by little mudholes were filled in, crooked turns straightened and bridges built. Towns were brought closer together and people were able to go visiting. Merchants could trade with each other and sell goods shipped from far-off places. Travelers crossed the country in "stage" coaches, called this because they made trips in "stages," changing to fresh horses at each stage.

Coachmakers built many kinds of beautiful, shining carriages for rich people. They had odd names, like cabriolets, victorias, hansoms, calèches and barouches. In the cities there were horse-drawn buses and streetcars. Rich sportsmen gave "Tally-ho" parties, taking their friends on cross-country trips aboard glittering coaches pulled by six or eight horses.

Still, not a coach, carriage or bus could move faster than a horse could trot, and even the strongest horse had to walk some of the time.

Then came the great change in transportation.

An Englishman named George Stephenson, using the wheel, of course, built a steam engine in 1829, and mounted it on wheels. This locomotive was powerful enough to pull a train of little cars along a track. Suddenly that six-mile-an-hour speed limit was boosted to twenty and even more. The railroad was so successful that a network of tracks soon covered the land. Now people and goods could be transported quickly over great distances, instead of remaining within a circle of no more than 50 miles.

Around 1900 a new kind of transportation appeared. This was the automobile, powered by the gasoline engine. It was soon to drive the horse-drawn buggy and wagon from the streets. Just as the stagecoach was put out of business by the railroad, and the horsecar by the electric trolley car, they in turn were replaced by the motorbus, the truck and the automobile.

Thousands of miles of wide, paved roads were built to carry the new traffic. Farmers who once were marooned on their farms by muddy roads in spring and deep snow in winter could now go to town any time. A trip which once took half a day by horse and buggy now shrank to half an hour by car. Anybody could get foods from far-off places.

POWER REPLACES THE HORSE

At top left we see an early 1830 steam loco-motive, which ran on wooden rails and burned chunks of pine in its firebox. Below is a later camel-type engine with only one drive wheel to a side. The woodbin was part of the engine. Top middle shows an early trolley car. The motor-man stood on an open front platform. In winter he had to wear a huge bearskin overcoat and hat plus ear muffs. At the right is a three-wheel motor carriage, and at bottom center a one-cylinder 1908 Cadillac.

10

MODERN TRANSPORT

Top left shows one of the last of the giant steam locomotives. They have been replaced by the new diesel oil-burning engines shown at bottom right. Top right shows a 600-mile-an-hour jet plane. In the center is one of the latest tractor-trailer rigs which can carry enormous loads of freight for thousands of miles. While the fast plane and the automobile are taking passengers from the trains, the motor truck is taking business from the freight train. Bottom left shows a modern 8-cylinder sports car.

The earliest boat was probably a floating log, found by some hairy hunter who had to cross a river to get home. We can imagine how he straddled the log and slowly headed for the opposite bank by splashing and paddling.

Later he found he could make better speed by poling the log with a broken-off sapling. He soon found that a pole was useless when the water got deep, so he split a piece of log to make a flat board, lashed a pole to it and found he had made the first paddle.

All over the world people made all sorts of poling, paddling or rowing boats. Some, called *coracles*, were simply animal bladders, blown full of air to make them float. In the South Seas the natives built tremendously long canoes out of hollowed-out logs. They lashed smaller logs called *outriggers* to the ends of poles fastened across the canoes. The outriggers kept them from tipping over, and the natives made trips of thousands of miles over the rough Pacific.

The Greeks and Romans used galleys which were propelled by rows of oars extending from their sides. Some had two or three rows of oars, one above the other, called *biremes* and *triremes*. The oars were pulled by galley slaves.

Boatmen had long used small sails to help them along when the wind was astern. Then the wheel was put to work at sea. When a small wheel was set into a block and suspended at the masthead, it became a pulley. A rope run through a pulley or block was much more powerful than a straight pull.

Wheels with their axles fastened to the deck were called *capstans*. When they were turned up by means of long levers the anchor cable would wind up and the heavy anchor be brought aboard. Next, steering wheels took the place of hard-to-handle tillers. With the help of the wheel, great clippers with towering masts and great clouds of sail were built.

Then the wheel, as part of the steam engine, drove the clippers and all other sailing ships from the oceans of the world in a few short years. A man named Robert Fulton built a boat named the *Clermont* on the Hudson River, and installed a steam engine which turned a pair of paddle wheels rigged outside the hull.

On August 7, 1830, the *Clermont* cast off her lines in New York and started her engine. As the paddles thrashed the water into foam the boat slowly moved out of the slip and headed up the river. *Clermont* made the 150-mile trip to Albany in 32 hours.

The wheel had made the steam engine possible, and so also the steamboat. Fulton's *Clermont* was followed by many other steamboats, especially on the rivers. In the 1830's the Middle West beyond the Allegheny Mountains was still a trackless wilderness. The trappers, farmers and lumbermen of the Ohio country couldn't send their products eastward over the roadless mountains, so they had to ship everything down the Ohio to the Mississippi and thence to New Orleans. The trouble was that while a flatboat or raft would float down the rivers, there was no way of getting it back up against the current.

The shallow paddle-wheel steamboat was the perfect answer. Soon every big river was swarming with puffing side-wheelers. It took much longer to design steamships to cross the Atlantic. In the first place, the paddle wheel which worked so well on the rivers was likely to be knocked to pieces by the first Atlantic gale. Then, too, the distances between ports were so much greater. A river boat could stop at a landing every few miles and load a few cords of wood for the furnaces. A steamship would have to carry fuel enough for a 3,000-mile voyage. So, for a long time, ocean steamships also were fully rigged with masts and sails and used their engines only when the wind died or was against them. The engines were so low-powered that the ships were very slow.

Year by year, better engines were built. Coal began to be used for fuel because it gave better heat and took up much less room than wood. The screw propeller was invented. It did its work at the end of a shaft under water at the stern, safe from high waves. Soon the paddle wheel for ocean packets disappeared. Now the day of the oil-burning superliner had arrived.

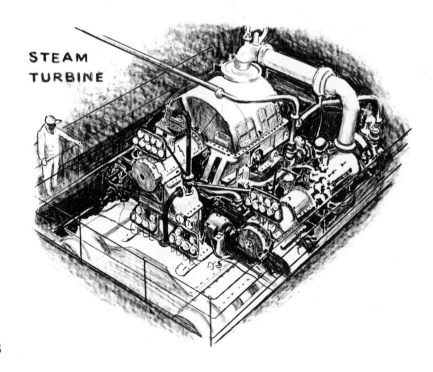

STEAM TURBINE

BEFORE THE WHEEL

This is how men had to sweat to drive their boats before they knew how to use the wheel. Top row shows, first, African natives poling their dugout canoe on a river in Guinea. Next is a Chinese river junk being poled and rowed on the Yangtse River. When these junks reach the gorges upriver, where the water foams down the steep rapids, they tie up along the bank. Then a network of ropes with one end fastened to the bow of the boat is laid out on the bank ahead. A gang of coolies takes hold of each rope and they all strain forward, hauling the boat up through the rapids. The bottom row shows a Roman corn ship rowed by a single row of oars, and some North American Indians in a birch-bark canoe.

THE WHEEL GOES TO SEA

Here we see what happened to ships after seamen learned to use the wheel. At the top left is an eighteenth-century East Indiaman with all sails set. You may ask what wheels have to do with a sailing ship. This one has a steering wheel, a capstan to raise the anchor, and hundreds of pulleys or blocks to handle and trim sail. Below the Indiaman is an early steam propeller ship. She still carries all her sails because sailors don't quite trust those early wood-burning engines. Top right shows the oil-burning, turbine-driven S. S. *United States*, fastest liner in the world. Below her is a modern diesel-powered tug, which keeps traffic moving in the harbor, towing barges and docking liners and cargo ships. At bottom right is a modern fishing yacht.

THE WHEEL AND COMMUNICATION

How do we communicate? The simplest way, of course, is by talking to each other, or by yelling if we're farther apart. This was the only way our ancestors, the early cave men, had.

Later, relays of runners or mounted messengers carried communications over long distances by memorizing a message and repeating it to each relay. Then, slowly, people began to find other ways. They sent signals by smoke during the day and by fires at night over long distances, as the Indians did. The early Greeks transmitted code messages by flashes from the sun reflected from their polished shields. At night signal torches or lanterns sent out information. Remember how Paul Revere learned whether the British were coming by land or by sea, from lanterns hung in the belfry of the old North Church in Boston?

In Africa the natives learned how to send long messages over great distances through the jungle by beating on drums. In France, Napoleon sent military orders over chains of semaphore stations, each one repeating the message to the next. At sea, naval vessels spelled out signals between them by means of strings of code flags flown from a masthead.

Another way of communication was opened when people learned how to draw and read signs and to read and write. The Chinese used carrier pigeons to deliver letters written on tissue and wrapped around the bird's leg. Finally people wrote letters to each other, delivered by servants or by postmen.

Another kind of communications was by means of written books. This had one big advantage. It didn't disappear like the spoken word or the smoke signal. It would still be there next week or next year, so that many people could use it for a long time.

There were drawbacks to all the ways. Carrying messages by runner or rider was very slow. The weather could keep one from seeing smoke or light signals for days. It was hard to send long messages that way. Books were fine, except that it took months for a monk, bending over a parchment with his quill pen, to copy one book.

Now let's see what the wheel did for communication. First, with improved roads everywhere, mail coaches delivered the mail faster and more regularly than did the old-time horseman. Then came the railroads whose fast mail trains speeded up postal delivery. Rotary printing presses were invented — the wheel again — and newspapers could be printed faster and cheaper than by the old flat-bed press. Books, too, were printed so cheaply that everybody could read them.

In 1843 came a new invention which was to give communication the speed of light. This was Samuel Morse's electric telegraph, made possible by the wheel. The electric generator which supplied the current, the machines which spun the fine copper wires, all needed wheels.

The telegraph was soon to span the oceans. The cable had to be laid by steamships, whose engines needed wheels. The cable was spun by wheeled wire-making machines.

Alexander G. Bell discovered how to send the human voice over a wire, and the telephone was born. Today our lives are so tied to the telephone that we could hardly get along without it.

On December 12, 1901, Guglielmo Marconi telegraphed words between England and America *without any wires at all*. Wireless telegraphy was especially wonderful for ships at sea.

The radio tube, invented by Fleming and DeForest, changed the clicks of the wireless to voice broadcasting. Soon radio was sending news, music, entertainment, weather reports, and education to any home that wanted it.

Next inventors began to work on a big tube which would do something almost unbelievable. It would send moving pictures through the air. Television had arrived. For years, of course, we already had the moving picture, whose cameras and projectors both needed wheels.

The latest wonderful steps in communication are the invention of radar, which paints an electric picture of what surrounds it, on a screen, even in fog, storm or darkness, and the rocket and space vehicle. From these we will soon learn what it is like to visit the moon and Mars.

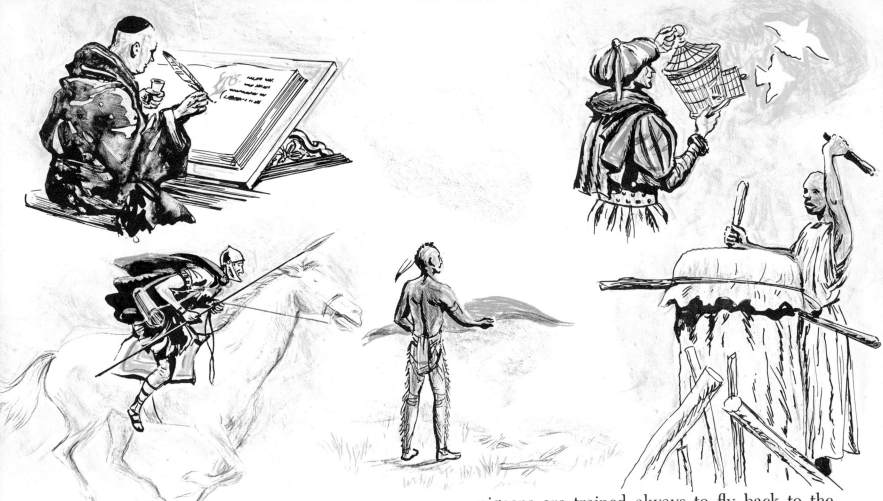

BEFORE THE WHEEL

Top row shows, first, a medieval monk copying Latin sentences into the parchment pages of a book. Next, a pigeon trainer releases birds carrying message scrolls tied to their legs. The pigeons are trained always to fly back to the home coop. Below, at left, is a mounted courier relaying a message. At the next stage he will pass it to another courier on a fresh horse. Next, an Indian is "talking" with smoke puffs from his signal fire to other Indians.

Last, an African drummer is beating out a message on a drum made of a hollow log.

THE WHEEL IN COMMUNICATION

Top left shows the mail coach, jouncing over the road to the shrill blast of the postman's horn.

Next across, we see a mail train of the 1860's. Bottom row shows a Morse sending key which clicks out telegraph messages. Above it is a jet plane which can carry a letter from New York to Paris in 6½ hours. Lower right shows a giant rotary newspaper press. Paper from a huge roll of newsprint is fed into one end. It whizzes between many rollers which print both sides of hundreds of pages so fast that the type is a blur as it passes through.

THE WHEEL AND FARMING

For many centuries farming was very hard work. The farmer had to do everything with his own muscles and a few tools. In the spring the ground had to be dug up with a spade, or plowed with a sharpened tree limb pulled by oxen or by the peasant's wife and children. Then the ground was broken up with hoes or crude, horse-drawn harrows. Next, the fields were seeded by tossing handfuls of seed from a bag tied over the peasant's shoulder as he trudged along the furrows. When the sprouts came up, there were endless days of weeding and hoeing, all by hand. When the crops were ripe there was more hard work. They had to be cut with small sickles, gathered together and tied in bundles by hand. Then the peasants carried the sheaves on their backs to the barns.

Hayfields were also cut with sickles. Then the hay was raked into piles with hand rakes and left to dry in the sun. When it was dry it was loaded in tall mounds on packs and carried on the farmers' backs to the haymow.

At threshing time, the bundles of wheat, oats and other grains were carried to the farmyard and beaten with a flail, a sort of hinged stick. This loosened the kernels on the stalks. Then when the wind was blowing hard, the farmer and his family picked up forkfuls of the grain and tossed them high in the air. The wind blew the light straw away while the kernels fell back to the ground, to be gathered in baskets and sacks.

Before the wheel, of course, there were no water or wind mills to grind the grain into flour. The women had to crush the kernels with a mortar and pestle. This was a hollowed log or stone into which the grain was poured, and a wooden or stone plunger to crush it.

When the wheel came to the farm, life grew easier for the peasant. At first wheels were used to make carts and wagons which were pulled by horses and oxen. Then blacksmiths began making improved plows and cultivators mounted on wheels. They were pulled by horses and saved many days of backbreaking toil with spade and hoe. Presently factories began to turn out wheeled, horse-drawn mowers and reapers which cut long swaths in the grain and hay fields. Soon the scythe and sickle disappeared. Horse-drawn binders were built, to gather the grain into bundles, bind them up and dump them into wagons. Once in the barn, they were fed into horse-powered threshing machines which beat the kernels out much faster than the flails could do it.

Instead of crushing the grain in a mortar, the farmer loaded the sacks aboard his wagon and took them to the nearby gristmill. Here the kernels were poured between two great slow-moving millstones which ground them into fine white flour. The stones were geared to a paddle wheel outside, which was turned by a stream of water pouring out of a chute from the dammed-up millpond. There was still much hand labor on the farm, but the wheel was making things easier.

It was when the wheel became part of the steam engine, the electric motor and the gas or diesel engine that things began to move fast on the farm. Great gang plows pulled by tractors plowed many furrows at once. They dragged harrows and rollers behind them, so that after the machine passed, the ground was ready for planting. Tractor-powered drills or seeders followed behind, dropping in the seeds automatically and covering the trench afterward. Motorized cultivators cleared out the weeds, and sprayers killed the insects.

At harvest time, enormous threshers called *combines* rolled across the wheat fields, cutting wide bands of the grain. It was carried up an endless belt into the machines where the kernels were separated and poured into sacks, while the straw was baled and dropped into trucks driving alongside. One such combine could cut and thresh hundreds of acres a day.

Motor corn pickers clattered across a cornfield, stripping the ears from the stalks, husking the ears, and tossing them into a trailer behind. Mowers cut the hay and baled it. Long-armed motor loaders picked up the bales and stacked them high in the hay barns. Now almost everything on the farm is mechanized. There are bean pickers, cotton pickers, potato pickers, and many others, all motor-powered to save hand labor.

Electric milking machines, cream separators, churns, all make life easier for the dairy farmer. Farms no longer depend on hand pumps or windmills for water. They have electric pumps to deliver running water everywhere, just as in the city. On western farms many farmers use their own private airplanes to get from one part of the farm to another and to crop-dust their fields from above to kill off insect pests. Today the wheel has changed the farm from a place of grinding hand labor to big business.

BEFORE THE WHEEL

This is farming before the wheel. At top you can see a peasant plowing with a sharpened tree limb. Next is a man chopping weeds with a hoe. At left, a man is sowing a field. Next is a haying scene; to the right, men are cutting grain with a sickle and binding the bundles. At bottom, harrowing with a drag made of logs.

22

THE WHEEL AND THE FARM

Here are just a few of the many power tools the modern farmer uses today. At top left is a disk gang plow hauled by a diesel tractor. Top right shows a hay grapple which bites out big chunks from a haystack and places them into a hayrack. Bottom left shows a corn picker at work, dropping the husked ears into the trailer truck behind. At right is a corn planter. It cultivates the ground ahead, plants four rows of corn and drops ammonia from a tank in front.

THE WHEEL AND MEAT

In the long-ago days before the wheel, meat came to the dinner table in a very different way. Today we simply go to the gleaming white counters and frozen-food bins at the supermarket. There we find waiting beef, pork, lamb, chickens, turkeys, sausages, all ready to be sliced in any amount by the butcher. His big refrigerator rooms are refilled every day with fresh meat. All of it has been inspected by government inspectors who stamp each carcass with a purple stamp to show the grade and freshness of the meat. Usually the meat has been trimmed of bones and extra fat. Chickens, ducks and turkeys have been plucked and cleaned.

Let's see what shopping for meat was like in the old days. First of all, there was no refrigeration, so meat would spoil very soon after butchering. This meant it had to be eaten at once. There was no quick way to get butchered meat from a farm many miles from town, so the animals had to furnish their own transportation. Cattle, pigs, sheep and geese were driven from the farms along the paths to the towns. There they were slaughtered and sold at once. A woman couldn't buy her meat whenever she liked. She had to wait for the town crier to an-

nounce a slaughtering at a certain hour. Even then she couldn't get beef or lamb on a day when only pigs were being butchered — she took what she could get. In times of heavy snow or deep mud she might not get any fresh meat at all.

Many people bought their meat "on the hoof" — alive. They butchered the animals themselves and made head cheese, sausages, smoked and pickled and salted meat. Fowls were usually bought alive, too. They were carried home squawking with their feet tied together. Then they had to be beheaded, plucked, scalded and cleaned before they could be cooked.

Before the railroads reached the Far West, ranchers in Texas and other western states could only get their cattle to market by driving them over the prairie and desert and across rivers. Surrounded by mounted cowboys, the herd would move slowly along one of the famous trails like the Santa Fe or the Oregon trail toward the railhead to the east.

They moved slowly because the cattle had to have time to graze every day. The big problem was to see that the herd reached water along the trail before the cattle died of thirst.

Even after the railroads were built and the

cattle were shipped in open-sided cars and fed and watered often, they arrived so exhausted and bruised that they lost a lot of weight. This meant that they were worth less money.

Refrigeration has changed everything in the meat business. Instead of shipping the animals long distances to stockyards in the East, they are put into a truck at the farm and delivered in a few hours to a stockyard nearby. After butchering, the meat is hung in chilling rooms until it is ready to be eaten. Then it goes to storage plants all over the country in refrigerator cars or trucks. Today a butcher can call the packing-house storage plant near his shop and order whatever he wants. In a few hours the truck stops at his back door and the sides of meat are carried into his own cooler. There they are cut up, packaged and put into the bins for the customers to select.

The wheel has made possible canning and freezing of meat and its swift transportation anywhere.

BEFORE THE WHEEL

Above we see an old-time farmer butchering a pig. After skinning it is scalded with hot water from the iron pot over the fire, and cut up. Everything is used. The hide is tanned and used to make belts and harnesses. Above, right, we see a cattle drive on the trail. The "dogies" are urged gently along, and allowed to graze along the way. At night they are herded together while the cowboys circle them, singing softly to keep them quiet. Below, a swineherd is driving a herd of grunting pigs from the farm where they were born and fattened, to be slaughtered.

THE WHEEL AND MEAT

This is how modern meat packers work. Above is a corner of one of the big chilling rooms in a packing plant. Carcasses of steers all ready for the butcher hang from hooks on an overhead rail line. An inspector is labeling the beeves with a roller marker. At right is a stock pen into which the cattle ready for market are driven. Railroad stock cars are run alongside the ramp and the animals are driven up the ramp into the car. Below is a big modern tractor-trailer rig. Its refrigerator plant keeps the trailer below freezing, so that the meat won't spoil before the truck gets it to the butcher shop.

**FOOD STORAGE BEFORE
THE WHEEL**

Before refrigeration every farm had to have a cold cellar and a springhouse. Sometimes they

were together. Everything from the garden, the orchard and the dairy had to be kept cool. Cabbages, turnips, pears and apples kept well in a cold cellar where the temperature never went down to 32 degrees.

Sometimes potatoes were stored in a straw-lined hole in the ground, well covered with earth. In the spring when the danger of freezing was over, they were dug up. Vegetables and fruits which wouldn't keep over the winter were preserved in glass jars. Sauerkraut, apple butter, pickles, pickled vegetables and some kinds of meat were packed in kegs, well salted down, or in big stone crocks. Hams, bacon and sausages hung from hooks in the ceiling to keep them out of reach of rats and mice.

These stored foods were good, but by the end of winter people had grown very tired of the lack of variety. As soon as the first green shoots of spring appeared they went out to dig up dandelions and tender fiddleback ferns for salad. The first radishes and green peas were eagerly awaited. Only what they themselves raised appeared on their tables. They never saw oranges, grapefruit, pineapples or avocados unless they lived where such fruit grew.

28

THE WHEEL BRINGS REFRIGERATION

Before modern refrigeration, ice cutters sawed great chunks of ice from the surfaces of ponds and rivers. These pieces were hauled into ice-houses and buried in sawdust to slow down melting. Ice was used for many years in butchers' iceboxes, in refrigerator freight cars and in home iceboxes. With ice, it was hard to keep the temperatures in boxes even, because as the ice melted, the box grew warmer. Besides, even a box filled to the top with ice couldn't *freeze* anything.

Then came electric refrigerators. They could be set for any temperature and they needed no iceman to fill the box every day. They could make ice themselves, and freeze food solid if desired. This led to a wonderful discovery. Scientists found that if foods were frozen very quickly ice crystals won't form in them. These crystals, formed when foods are slow-frozen, tore the little flavor cells in food. When it was defrosted the flavor leaked out and spoiled the taste. Quick-frozen foods could be stored for months and still tasted fresh when thawed. Now we can have all the delicate, out-of-season fruits and vegetables and any kind of meat at any time at stores with frozen-food counters.

FISHING — BEFORE THE WHEEL

Fishing is one of the oldest ways of getting food. In thousands of years fishing methods have changed very little. Fish were speared, caught with a hook and line, or netted. Here we see a purse seine being hauled, in ancient times. The fishermen have no wheels to help them; there is no machinery aboard their boats. All the work is done with their own muscle power.

The two boats have rowed out to sea, watching gulls and other birds for signs of a school of fish below. When they see the birds clustering and swooping down, one boat holds one end of the net. The other boat makes a wide circle, paying out net as it goes, and returns to the first boat, where the two ends are tied together. Now the net hangs down in a circle, like a fence under water.

Now a rope run through the bottom of the net like a drawstring is pulled until the bottom is closed. The net is like a giant purse, and any fish inside are imprisoned. The two boats lie opposite each other, each with a side of the net tied to the gunwale. The men begin to haul in, a little at a time. They can see the frantic flashes below, and soon fish begin to leap out of the water. The net gets heavier and heavier and the men strain and heave. At last the purse end is a solid mass of flapping fish, and the men scoop them out with long-handled nets and toss them into the boats. When they have a load they must race for shore before the catch spoils.

THE WHEEL AND MODERN FISHING

A modern fishing boat is a mass of wheels and machinery. Besides its powerful engine, it has big winches driven by motors, which haul in the net. It carries radar and radio and ship-to-shore telephone. The fishing boat we see here is called a dragger. It lets down an enormous net shaped like a bag. Tough cowhides are sewn to the bottom to keep the net from being torn as it is dragged along the rough ocean floor. The mouth of the net has weights sewn to the bottom, and floats across the top to keep it open.

At each end is a wooden "door" rigged at an angle to the dragrope. When the ship is moving, the force of the water pushes the doors apart and keeps the mouth of the net stretched wide.

The dragger steams slowly along, pulling the net along the bottom and scooping up whatever fish it comes upon. When the captain thinks he has a haul, the winches start winding up the cable and the net is brought alongside, hoisted above the hatches and opened to dump the catch into the fish well.

The earliest men probably wore no clothes at all. They had long hair all over their bodies to keep them warm. Later, prehistoric men began to look more like us. They had less hair and so they needed protection from the cold. Of course they had no way of making cloth, so they wore the skins of animals they had killed, the bark of trees and leaves of plants.

If we examine our North American Indians, we can get a good idea of the way early man dressed. When an Indian killed a deer he skinned it and turned it over to his squaw. She carefully scraped it clean of meat and fat and then pegged it to a frame to dry and cure. To make it soft and pliable the squaw had to chew every bit of the skin. Afterward she cut it to the shape of a shirt or leggings and sewed it with sinews saved from the deer's butchering.

The hand loom was the first machine to weave cloth. Before the wheel, the threads used in the loom were spun between the palms of the hands. It was slow work and the threads were uneven, so the cloth woven from such thread was rough and uneven, too.

Every stitch of sewing had to be done by hand because there were no sewing machines before the wheel. Stockings and mufflers were knitted by hand with knitting needles. Old women spent much of their time knitting — it took a long time to make a pair of stockings.

Shoemakers also had to do their work by hand. They cut out the leather with a sharp knife, punched holes in it with an awl and sewed the parts of the shoe together with waxed thread. The soles were fastened on with tiny wooden pegs. The journeyman shoemaker traveled from farm to farm, visiting each place once a year. While he was there he would measure each member of the family and make a new pair of shoes for each one. Clothes and shoes in the early days were made heavy and strong, to last a long time. People didn't buy new clothes just because the old ones were out of fashion.

Then the spinning wheel was invented, and clothmaking became easier. With the wheel a woman could spin strong, even thread from hanks of flax, wool or cotton. It was much faster than the old hand way. The loom was improved too. Inventors found ways of applying the wheel to weaving machines, and soon they were run by water or steam power. The machines spun thread and wove cloth automatically. The mill hands had only to feed in fresh bobbins of thread and see that the machines were working

right. Mills got bigger and bigger; many hundreds of men and women were needed to tend the long rows of clacking machines.

The wheel turned up again in the newly invented sewing machine. This brought a great change in clothes making. Before it, almost all clothes were made to order by a tailor, sitting cross-legged on the table in his little shop. Because every stitch was made by hand it took a long time to make a suit of clothes, so clothes were very expensive.

With the sewing machine a shirt could be made in less than an hour; by hand it took 13½

hours. A hand-sewn frock coat needed 17 hours. With the machine it took less than three. Now women could make their own clothes at home much faster with a home machine.

New machines were built presently which could turn out clothing even faster and better. Cutting machines could cut out fifty thicknesses of cloth from one pattern and the factory made fifty suits in the same time a hand tailor made only one. Ready-mades were made in all sizes so anyone could find a suit to fit him. One could walk out of a store with a suit in a box under one's arm, and the suit was cheaper than a handmade one. New knitting machines took over Grandma's job. They turned out underwear and stockings many times faster than her knitting needles could.

Next, the wheel began to take over the old-fashioned shoemaker's job. Shoe machines could cut out shoe lasts and uppers by the thousands while others sewed them together. Shoe factories made shoes in all sizes to fit anybody in many different styles.

Instead of small shops where one man made a suit or a pair of shoes to order, there were now big stores which didn't make the things they sold, but bought them from the big factories.

BEFORE THE WHEEL

At upper left a woman is working before an old-style hand loom on the island of Cyprus. The threads running in one direction are called the warp, those that cross them the woof. The cloth is woven, one thread at a time, by the patient weaver. To the right we see a couple of tailors sitting cross-legged as they cut and stitch.

All tailors, whether they lived in Germany or Egypt, sat like this at their work. Far right shows an old-fashioned shoemaker pegging a sole to the upper of a shoe. He could make you a pair of dancing slippers or a pair of heavy riding boots to your measure — if you gave him lots of time.

THE WHEEL AND TODAY'S CLOTHES

At top center you can see what started the revolution in clothes making — the spinning wheel. The old lady makes the wheel turn with a foot treadle while she feeds the hank of yarn into the spindle which twists it into thread. At left are a modern spinning machine and a loom weaving a roll of cloth. At right a shoe machine operator is stitching shoes together.

MINING BEFORE THE WHEEL

We know that men used gold, silver, copper and iron as far back as 4500 B. C. Tools and ornaments made of these metals have been found in Egyptian tombs. The Chinese and even the American Indians used metal. How did the early men get their metals? Geologists believe that they found them as nuggets, washed out of ore veins by the rain, or as meteorites. Meteorites are those fiery lumps of blazing matter we see shooting across the sky at night which we call shooting stars. Some of them crash into the earth and are made of a kind of iron.

Later, men discovered that the metals were found mixed with rock in ore veins under the ground. They began digging shafts and tunnels to uncover these veins. Without wheels those early mines were very crude. The miners had to climb up and down the shafts on notched logs for ladders. Down below they loosened the ore chunks with crude picks and hammers with stone or iron heads. They loaded the ore into baskets and carried them strapped to their backs up the notched logs. Later they hauled the baskets up by ropes. Probably the first wheel used in mining was a windlass to wind up the rope tied to an ore basket.

As mine tunnels grew longer, tracks were laid and little cars pulled by mules carried the ore to the shaft.

MINING AND THE MACHINE

In the twentieth century the wheel really went to work in the mine. Electric engines replaced the mine mule. Pneumatic drills and chain saws took the place of the hand drill and the sledge hammer. The hand scoop shovel was discarded in favor of the automatic loader. Below, left, an automatic caterpillar-tread loader is at work. After the pneumatic drill has bored holes which are filled with dynamite and exploded, huge chunks of ore fall to the floor of the tunnel. The scoop in the front of the loader is pushed under the pile of ore and an endless belt carries the chunks back to a chute. Then they fall from the end of the chute into the ore car which will carry them back to the shaft. At

right is a gigantic power shovel. When an ore vein is just below the surface, the big shovel strips off the earth and sand covering the vein. Then it scoops up the ore and loads it into enormous ore trucks to be taken to the smelter.

OIL BEFORE THE WHEEL

The thick, greenish-black liquid called petroleum was known for a long time, but until just a hundred years ago it was found only as a kind of scum floating on the surface of certain streams. Nobody really knew where it came from or how it reached the streams.

The Indians used to scoop it up from the streams in clamshells and use it as a medicine. When the white man arrived he copied the Indians. Then somebody found a much wider use for petroleum. When it was heated a clear liquid called kerosene could be separated from it. Kerosene would burn in a lamp with a wick and give off a much brighter light than candles or whale-oil lamps which were the only lights people had.

A man named Colonel Drake believed that petroleum came from underground and that it could be brought up by drilling a hole just as for water, only deeper. Here the wheel makes its bow. Colonel Drake went to Titusville, Pennsylvania, where surface oil seepage had been noticed. He bought a well-drilling rig which needed wheels to make the drill work, and began to drive a well. At first he struck water, then his hole filled with mud. He kept on until one day he found a black fluid rising in the well pipe. He had struck oil!

In a short time well derricks were rising everywhere. Soon more oil was being pumped up than could be burned in all the lamps of America. Just when it seemed that the oil business was done for, a new discovery saved it. Inventors had long been tinkering with a machine with a long name, the internal combustion engine. Several had been mounted in carriages and connected to the wheels. Sure enough, the new engine drove the horseless carriages. The automobile was born. These engines ran on gasoline, a by-product of petroleum left over when kerosene was refined. It had always been thrown away as useless. Now suddenly gasoline had become precious and the oil business boomed.

More and more uses were found for oil. It was used not only to run automobiles and trucks, but also railroad trains and ships. Homes were heated with oil instead of coal. Factories heated their boilers with it and steel mills their furnaces. The demand grew and grew.

Oilmen had to drill deeper and deeper to find new oil pools. They set up great platforms miles out to sea, to drill for oil under the ocean. Some drill rigs bored holes miles deep, others drilled at a slant. It took powerful engines to turn the drills and to raise and lower strings of tools and casing in such deep holes. Enormous trucks were needed to carry the drill rigs from field to field and to carry the pipe and all the other supplies a well needed.

While the wells were getting deeper, refining plants where the oil was separated into many different products grew larger and more complicated. At first refiners only wanted kerosene; they thought everything else was waste. Today the crude oil is boiled and its vapors floated up tall sealed towers. The lightest vapors float to the top of the tower where they cool into a liquid again and become gasoline. Heavier ones become liquid lower down, in a tray below the gasoline, to become kerosene. Still lower, lubricating oils and fuel oils are formed. At the bottom the heavy tars and asphalt gather.

Tank cars, motor barges and tank trucks, as well as seagoing tankers, distribute these products to factories, gas stations and homes.

MANUFACTURING BEFORE THE WHEEL

Before the wheel everything was made by hand. Tools were crude and simple. Craftsmen turned out fine and beautiful things but they were made one at a time and took a long time to finish. Mass production was unknown.

A cutler or swordmaker hammered away on a blade, patiently reheating it and tempering it in a tub of water, then hammering again for many days. The blacksmith forged hinges and locks on his small anvil while an apprentice pumped the hand bellows to make the fire burn hotter.

Here we see a group of handcraftsmen making brass vessels and trays. The man at the left is working a bow drill. As it moves back and forth like a fiddle bow, the string wound around the spindle whirls the drill. The next man is sawing out the pattern of a vase with a little handsaw.

Now the wheel enters manufacturing. Soon artisans have hand lathes turned by foot power. Then come drills, saws and lathes belt-driven from shafts turned by water wheels. Year by year new machines now driven by electricity do things better and faster with less hand labor. Workmen can turn out more work and so get higher pay. Railroad engines, steamships, traveling cranes, steel plants, skyscrapers, all are now possible.

40

THE WHEEL AND THE FACTORY

Now it is the middle of the twentieth century and the engineers have designed such marvelous automatic machines that they do their several jobs without men to guide them. The age of mass production is here. Engineers constantly study the machines to find ways of making products better and cheaper.

Now we are entering the automation era. Machines are now being built which can almost think for themselves. They can be set to solve their own problems. Only a few men will be needed to oversee them. Wheels of every kind are needed in automation.

Many factories have production lines. The product is hooked on at the beginning of the line and moves slowly through the factory. Along the line men assemble it. At the end of the line the complete product comes off, ready to ship.

The picture shows the assembly line of a great automobile factory. Chassis No. 1,784,010 already has its axles and wheels. The engine has been bolted in place, brakes and transmission connected, steering wheel put on. Now a complete body slides down from overhead rails. It has been pressed out of flat sheets of steel in an enormous body press. From there it went to the paint shop to be sprayed with paint and

then into an oven to bake the paint. Afterward doors and windows were added, upholsterers trimmed the inside, added seats and carpets. Now it is being lowered onto the chassis.

All the while, the endless belt assembly line has been slowly moving the chassis through the plant. Ahead, there are hundreds of cars a little more complete. Behind, hundreds more are waiting their turns for bodies. Almost everything in the great factory depends on the wheel.

BUILDING BEFORE THE WHEEL

At top left is a Plains Indian skin tepee. To pitch it a bundle of lodgepoles are leaned against each other in the shape of a cone, and tied at the top. Then the skins are wrapped around the cone, with a flap at the top left open for the smoke of the campfire to escape. Next is the log cabin of the backwoods frontiersman. Only an ax was needed to build it. Next is a tropical hut of bamboo poles lashed together and thatched with palm leaves. Lower right shows ancient Egyptians hauling part of a temple pillar on a sledge. At far right is an Eskimo winter hut built of blocks of snow.

THE WHEEL AND CONSTRUCTION

The tall building was made possible only when the elevator was invented, so that people could get to the upper floors without impossible climbing. It also had to wait for the steel mills to make steel beams and for factories to build cranes and hoisting machinery. The wheel plays a part in every stage of the skyscraper. At the beginning, big power shovels scoop out the foundation hole while giant trucks haul the dirt away. Cement for the foundations comes to the site in trucks which mix the cement in revolving drums while they drive from the cement plant. Other giant trucks bring the steel beams and turn them over to the giant cranes to lift them to the next floor to be erected. Temporary construction elevators haul up bricks, window frames, flooring, radiators, and all the thousands of other things which make up a modern building.

THE WHEEL IN WARFARE

Our savage ancestors waged war with clubs and stones for a long time. Then they sharpened poles to make spears and tied sharp-edged stones to clubs to make axes. Until the bow and arrow were invented they had to get pretty close to an enemy to hurt him.

For a long time the bow, the sword, and the battle-ax and spear were the only weapons of war. Armorers tried hard to invent defenses against them. They forged iron helmets and heavy leather iron-studded armor. They built shields, either of thick hides stretched over wooden frames, or of thin steel plates. They improved on the leather armor by constructing suits of mail made up of tiny steel links forged together, called *chain mail*.

Then the crossbow was invented. By cranking back a stiff steel bow, the crossbow got so much power that it could send a heavy steel arrow right through a shield or a hauberk of chain mail. To catch up, the armorers built entire suits of steel plates, jointed at arms and legs. For a time a mounted knight in plate armor could defeat anything.

The medieval castle was built to withstand any but the strongest attack. It had turrets and battlements from which bowmen and spearmen could

pour down clouds of steel shafts. From overhanging hoardings atop the walls, molten lead and boiling water could be poured on any enemy man-at-arms who got close to the base of the walls. Surrounding them was usually a deep ditch or moat filled with water. Heavy iron-plated doors and steel-barred portcullises barred the gateway, and the drawbridge over the moat was pulled up at the first sign of danger.

An army besieging such a castle built great siege engines of heavy wooden beams, which would heave great stones against the walls or send heavy darts over them. These machines of war were called *ballista, mangonels* and *catapults.* The attackers tried to fill the moat with stones and bundles of brush so that they could push lofty siege towers on rollers up to the walls. The towers had platforms on top overlooking the walls, from which archers shot down onto the garrison. When the tower approached the walls, mailed knights climbed ladders in the rear and leaped down on the battlements, swinging their great swords. Behind the siege machines stood squads of laddermen, waiting to rush forward and raise the ladders.

Then came the invention of gunpowder. It soon brought an end to the stone-walled castle, the armored knight and the crossbowman. Cannon could batter down any stone wall and the musket bullet far outranged the arrow and pierced the heaviest plate armor. This was the day of the muzzle-loading musket and the smoothbore cannon. At sea, ships of the line carried as many as 120 cannon.

Our terrible Civil War brought great changes to the art of warfare. The machine age was just beginning, with the wheel more and more important. Inventors used their new tools to design more and more powerful weapons. The famous duel between the *Monitor* and the *Merrimac* showed that the sailing warship was finished. Bigger cannon were built and their bores were rifled or grooved so that the shell would spin as it left the muzzle. This made it shoot straighter and farther. The muzzle-loading musket, which took several minutes to reload, was replaced by the breech-loading rifle which fired a cartridge. The repeating rifle soon followed, then the machine gun and the rapid-fire cannon.

Another war, World War I, brought another surge of military inventions. For the first time the airplane was used in battle. The first fighting planes shot at each other with pistols and shotguns, but they soon mounted machine guns in their ships. The first slow, clumsy bombers began to drop their fiery eggs. The British unleashed a new surprise on the Germans — the first armored tanks. These moved on caterpillar treads but the treads traveled on small wheels.

World War II brought still more improved weapons, longer-range guns, faster, deadlier planes, more powerful tanks. Finally the atomic bomb made warfare a million times deadlier.

BEFORE THE WHEEL

At left rides a knight upon his great war horse. He wears full armor plate, with a visored helmet. He swings a great long-sword. Next, a siege machine is being cranked. When the trigger is released it will hurl the great stone high. At right are a man-at-arms with a halberd, a longbowman and a crossbowman.

Here are three deadly instruments of modern warfare. At the top is a jet-powered, needle-nosed fighter plane. Lower left shows a tank crashing through the jungle to attack. Lower right shows a short-range rocket, launched from a truck. This rocket can deliver an atomic war head.

THE WHEEL AND MODERN WEAPONS